Mongolian Interior
AN EXPATRIATE EXPERIENCE

LORI YOUNKER

Cover and illustrations by
LAUREL SPRENGER

2017

Printed in the United States of America

First Printing, 2017
CreateSpace

ISBN-13: 978-1546997344

ISBN-10: 1546997342

Contact Lori Younker at lori@worldsobright.org
www.WorldSoBright.org

Dedicated to

Peter, Joanna, and Mary
who withstood the worst
and came out for the best

and

Laurel Sprenger
who gave color and light to my memories

Our work in Mongolian would not have been possible without the faithful support and encouragement from our monthly financial supports.

This book is also for them.

CONTENTS

Introduction 1

Poem: *Lord of the Sky* 3

I. Strong Sense of Direction 5

II. Escape 13

III. In Search of Light 21

IV. Looking Back 29

V. Giving Haircuts by Candlelight 41

VI. Where Fahrenheit Meets Celsius 51

VII. Pushing Uphill 61

VIII. Go with the Flow 73

IX. Returning 83

APPENDIX

Twelve Stones 95

The Mongolian Hillbillies 97

Special Thanks 99

Biographical Information 101

Introduction

In 1992, my husband Bill and I served a small congregation in Winner, South Dakota where we heard about a delegation of Dakotans that traveled to Mongolia as agricultural experts for grassland concerns. Mongolia, formerly known as the Mongolian People's Republic, had severed Soviet ties and were forging a new democracy.

This delegation was given a tour of the legislative buildings when they were invited into the auditorium. Freedom of religion was the topic of discussion and the visitors were urged to give their opinion on the matter. Without preparation, they briefly listed economic and societal benefits for the nation that ensures human rights for its people. Before they left for home— if our information is correct—freedom of religion was written into the constitution.

Reports of their serendipitous visit intrigued us. Soon, my husband Bill and I took our three children (Peter, Joanna, and Mary) to do our part in the transformation of the Mongolian society. When we arrived, the population was 2.2 million people with only three Christian churches in existence. Upon our return to the States five years later, the number of believers was estimated at 30,000.

Professional Resources Group International developed a micro-business enterprise which trained Mongolians in independent businesses under the leadership of Tom Suchy. The physical product was Bubbling Springs, a 12,000 sq. foot multi-purpose building located in the Bayanzurkh area of the 13th micro-district of Ulaanbaatar.

Counting churches is one thing; the training and personal growth of the first believers and their families is much harder to measure. We only know our hearts are full and bubbling over with memories seventeen years later.

We would like to believe, especially as American Christians, that we would offer all kinds of wonderful deeds for the Mongolian people. However, expectations were hindered drastically by language difficulties, the political climate, homeschooling responsibilities, and daily chores, just to name a few.

The first recorded missionary to Mongolia, James Gilmour spoke of these daily obstacles in his diary which describes his itinerant preaching on the Mongol steppes in the early 1880s,

> *Another week has passed over my head with many hopes and fears. In many points of my journey I expected difficulties which might have stopped me short in my path, but all these have disappeared, and I am here, having succeeded beyond expectations. One thing is not right: my readiness to forget the ways God has helped me...In this manner I am not only guilty of ingratitude, but lose much joy and strength of faith and hope.* ---James Gilmour, from *Among the Mongols*

In the same way, Bill and I persevered through each day's challenges with the knowledge that God was sustaining us with a song in our hearts or a faint, yet continual, sense that everything would be "okay."

Through the love of generous Mongolians, we lived as expats in the capital city of Ulaanbaatar from 1995 to 2000 with men and women and their families from the U.S.A., Canada, England, South Africa, Germany, Sweden, South Korea, Switzerland, Finland, and Hungary. Some stayed on. Some returned. Some call Mongolia their home. I hope these stories speak for us all.

–Lori Younker, May 2017

LORD OF THE SKY

Tenghir Minh
My great Lord of the blue sky
Heal our Mongol nation's heart
Absorbed by melodious tones
Let us devote our hearts
And lives to you.

Long ago, our ancestors
Used to call out, "Lord of the Sky!"
We of this future generation
Will begin to truly know and call you
Our "Lord of the Sky!"

Show compassion on our Mongolia!
Bless our nation
Renew our vast steppes we pray.
May all of Mongolia
Worship only you.

We will worship you
On our knees, we'll bow down
And humbly pray.

Composed by Mongolian Christians
of the copper mining city of Erdenet, circa 1995-97

Strong Sense of Direction

Peter in the capital city of Ulaanbaatar
3rd & 4th District
May 1995

Pete keeps his head down, alert for large rocks and broken bottles. He kicks the dust to watch it fly out from his feet. He swerves past several lengths of rusted rebar that protrude from the troubled earth and uses them as markers to find his way back to the apartment. Above him tower several apartment buildings, the concrete dinosaurs of the Soviet past, and he finds a narrow footpath between two.

A few yards from Building 66, Entrance Number 4, he feels blood oozing down the side of his face. He touches the place where the rock hit him above the eyebrow. *Let it drip,* he thinks. His mother and father should see how the boys here make friends.

He passes an old woman whose head is covered with a purple kerchief, her face tan, shiny, and weathered. She is perched on the bank of the hill near the door with a cardboard box at her side. "Potatoes!" she calls with music in her voice and raises a large potato high in the air. But, she sees it's the American boy and places it back into the box.

Pete reaches for the handle of the heavy, metal door. He reads the black letters in Cyrillic letters, certain the words do not say, "Welcome."

Braced for the acrid smell of urine, it shocks him anyway, and the door bangs loudly behind him like the sound of prison bars.

He counts the flights of stairs with labored steps, and on the sixth floor, he presses the doorbell and waits for a family member to let him in, thinking it's about time he had his own key.

Inside, his little sister Mary badgers him with questions. "What's wrong? Are you okay?"

She's clueless to the pains of this world, sheltered under Mother's skirts. She has no idea what it's like to be a boy.

While he sits on a wooden stool in the kitchen, Mother wipes the blood from his face with a washcloth dipped in warm water, and squeezes the details out of him.

"They got their message across. That's for sure," he tells her.

In his room, he flings himself on his Colorado Rockies bedspread and reminds himself of the decision he made shortly after arriving in the country. He will not cry. His toes feel the edge of his bed, and he slides them back and forth, recounting several opportunities where he might have abandoned his resolve. Take for example, yesterday, when he led his mother and sisters to the river bottoms near the bridge. There, a small gang of teenagers taunted them with names like "Ruuski" and "outsider."

"We're American!" he yelled out in broken Mongolian.

The teens marched in closer, forcing his mother and sisters to retreat toward the cement walls that lined this part of the river, leaving no escape.

One boy pulled out a switchblade. Pete flung his arms open wide to shield his mother and tried again, "Leave us alone! We're not Russians."

With his tirade complete, the gang strutted away flinging rocks as parting gifts. Then Pete shepherded his mother and sisters back to the apartment.

Now safe on his bed, he reassures himself that he has dodged

any real danger and falls asleep. A few hours pass when the doorbell announces that some children have come to see the American boy. They are ushered into the main corridor of their apartment. With no light fixtures in the ceiling, they stand in the shadows.

Pete's little sister makes the introduction. "My friend from the third floor brought her friends. They want to play with you."

From his bedroom door, Pete watches three boys in black leather jackets and jeans jostle for position. One steps forward, another step back. He eyes the boys with doubt and keeps his lips tight.

In the emptiness of their exchange, he remembers a similar encounter back in South Dakota when he visited a ranch with his father. He was the newbie from Chicago, and the local boys born and bred on the plains had sized him up from under their cowboy hats. Pete had hoped for a tour of the barn and the out-buildings, and if he was lucky, he might even get a ride on a horse. Those hopes disappeared quickly, aware of his own attire, his T-shirt, tennis shoes and shorts. Why hadn't he worn jeans?

Now in the corridor, Mary's friend picks up the loose ends of the conversation with a little English, "My brother want show you shop. You want?"

Pete reads their body language. One looks him in the eye, nodding and smiling. He thinks he sees in this boy a measure of sincerity, so he lifts his chin in agreement and puts on his shoes.

His mother calls from the kitchen, "Don't go too far."

"I know how to get home. Don't worry."

Pete has always been good at directions. In fact, he takes pride in his ability to know where he is at all times. When he was just four years old, he could direct the family from their home to K-mart. He knows all the turns to his grandparent's cabin in Colorado, every twist on the mountain pass.

These boys want to show him the shops and the new supply

of backpacks from the Eastern Bloc. They descend the stairs quickly and reach the main shopping area without much effort. The oldest one is the most attentive to Pete. He points out where they will go next and pulls on his sleeve to direct him, urging him to keep up.

The shops are a labyrinth of glass counters filled with small items and walls covered in women's blouses. Through one hallway and then another, they dodge the crowded shoppers and avoid tripping over stacks of toilet paper, passing from one shop to another by mysterious doorways and a short flight of stairs painted in bright blue. Pete has his eye out for the backpacks.

They come to a large open plaza under the sky. Suddenly,

from his left, a man slaps a heavy hindquarter, a mass of startling red flesh onto a wooden counter, and Pete jumps. Elderly men are bidding for the meat.

He recognizes the numbers he hears, but he can't find the boys. His heart sinks. They have left him to fend for himself.

Pete is totally unaware that these boys are engaging in a rite of passage. Only trained and hearty men withstand the brutal nature of Mongolian life.

The oldest makes a suggestion, "Let's leave the silly American with his stupid Nikes ® and see if he can find his way back on his own."

One boy hesitates, "Do you think he'll be okay?"

"He'll be fine. Come on!" another says, and they dart through the crowd in a zigzag path around the side of the nearest building.

Pete finds the sidewalk along the Big Ring Road and is comforted by the familiar screech of the trolley passing by. He imagines the boys watch him from a nearly balcony, laughing, pointing at the American boy. His anger boils.

He digs into his pocket for the bus fare to the Urguu Kino Theater, a remarkable landmark of his neighborhood. One hundred *tughrik* will be enough. It's true he could walk, but it feels empowering to use the local transportation. So, he crosses the street to the bus stop on the other side.

On the trolley, he stations himself closest to the door and watches the shops pass with his nose against the glass. One of them surely holds the promised backpack, but he will save that mission for another day and will get back to his family. When the vehicle lurches to a stop, he disembarks under the tall, ornate building with its ancient script of gold metalwork comforts him.

He's nearly home.

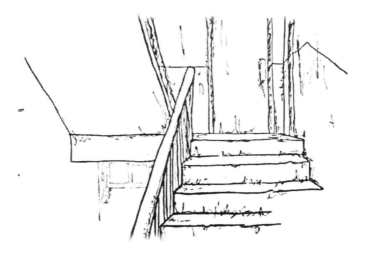

Inside Building 66, on his rush up the stairs to his apartment, he pauses to look out the window. He can see the sun casting a warm glow on the upper floors of the building to the north. With its light blue, chalk-painted surface, he is surprised how closely this view resembles the watercolor paintings for sale at Sukhbaatar Square. He blinks away salty tears which dry quickly on his cheeks, leaving a prickly sensation. He turns away from the window and runs a sleeve across his face.

A young mother is descending the steps with a little boy, so he shifts to the right to let them pass. She nods at him, and he manages to smile.

Watching their descent, something like a multiple-choice question runs through his mind. Option A: fight this place and be miserable. Option B: accept it bravely with its possibility of adventure. He grips the cold metal of the handrail, and somewhere between the fifth and the sixth floor, he makes his choice and climbs the remaining steps three by three.

On the sixth floor, he smells the delicious aroma of roasted beef with onions wafting from the apartment and presses the doorbell.

A man learns to keep things to himself.

Mary holds the door wide open. He's genuinely glad to see her, straightens his body as tall as it will go and announces his return, "Hey everybody, I'm home!"

Escape

Bayan Buural (Grey Head) Railroad Workers Resort
January 1996

When smoke filled the stairwell and slipped under the apartment doors, the Tuktaway family was huddled in their living room on the sixth floor, high above the ice-covered city of Ulaanbaatar. The three Tuktaway children fought over who would sit closest to the heater, when the second daughter began to cough and wheeze.

"Do you smell smoke?" Mother said with alarm.

Father jumped up from the sofa and opened the door of their little sanctuary just wide enough for his body to squeeze through the gap. "I'll go check," he said.

Holding his nose and face with a wet cloth, he followed the smoke and found its source. Flames rose from the massive pile of refuse at the bottom of the cavernous, six-story shaft in which the families, who called this building their home, dropped their trash.

A man who passed him on the stairs spoke to him in tones as flat as wooden planks, "Some kids lit the trash on fire. It happens all the time."

As the smoke grew thick and dark, Father knew he had to do something. This fire could burn for days and kill his asthmatic daughter. So, he lugged bucket after bucket of water from his apartment on the top floor to the garbage chute on the second, until he realized he had made the smoke worse.

Family Tuktaway took a walk. They described their predicament to their native friend Dash, and plans for a weekend at the Bayan Buural Railroad Union Resort took shape. Dash made arrangements for passenger train tickets and lodging at Bayan Buurral, affectionately translated as Gray Head Mountain.

"The name honors retired railroad workers," Mother told the children. "Let's wait out the fire there, far away from everything."

And so it was agreed that Dash would escort them to the resort. The Tuktaway family packed their bags and bundled themselves up to their noses in down-filled parkas and thick wool scarves. Wearing three pairs of socks a piece inside their Sorrel ® boots, the family 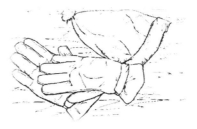 of five disembarked the train lumbering like sleepy bears.

Adjacent to the train station, the resort sat peacefully in a bed of snow. It was an asymmetric building, a cross between a spaceship and a cement version of a Frank Lloyd Wright. As the sun set, they posed for a photograph at the entrance, and Dash returned to his family on a train bound for the city.

The foyer was dark and wide. The floor creaked beneath their feet, and the older son surveyed the mosaic of narrow hardwood strips that had been painted a cheery yellow, scratched and bruised from decades of use. The hall stretched before them, and hiding in the shadows was a pool table. However, the oldest child knew that if the clerk who controlled the key for the storage closet wasn't on duty there would be no games.

"Look Mother, I can see my breath," the youngest daughter announced, and Mother, who hoped for a true retreat, began to doubt.

The first stop was the dining room, a large mess hall with camp-style tables and benches. A meal of gray noodles, meat, and onions was presented, accompanied by a huge kettle of hot water for tea. The sticky nature of the vinyl tablecloth was duly noted, and the bottom of their stomachs welcomed the hot meal.

Next, they were taken to their room, a Siberian prison cell with a door that didn't lock, a cement cubicle with red, paper-

thin carpet and two windows frosted both inside and out. It was quite apparent that every room of the resort was colder than home, and they climbed onto

the rock-hard beds in their parkas and boots to watch the steam of their own breath in front of their faces as they fell asleep.

Breakfast was millet porridge. Lunch was fried rice with little bits of meat and onion, and supper was gray noodles with chopped mutton and cabbage in a tasty, yet oily broth. Dessert was the family's first taste of *aaruul*, a treat made from mare's milk yoghurt.

"It's too sour," the youngest Tuktaway said with a grimace.

The out-of-doors made up for everything. Beyond the resort, two feet of snow was as fluffy as northern Michigan's. Every pine tree was laden with the white that makes the Alps famous. The family trekked to the top of the mountain behind the resort and found a genuine log home. The three Tuktaway children rolled like snowballs, tumbled and rough-housed through the merry woods with the parents following close behind. They all sweat in their heavy clothing and unzipped their parkas for a breeze.

On the highest point, the family looked out over the village to the south where the railway families lived. Father thought there might be a store where they could buy candy bars or a package of shortbread cookies.

With this idea, Mother fell silent. The snow had a strange effect on her. As each hour passed, she felt more and more insulated from this strange world called Mongolia, more distracted and protective of her own fragile psyche. She wasn't used to living so close to the dangers of cold and starvation, and this trip to the resort amplified the reality of their new existence.

The next day, the family marched through the snow to the small village of Bayan Buural, a collection of wooden buildings and traditional yurts. Smoke rose from the rooftops with the promise of warmth and friendship. However, Mother hit an imaginary wall about two hundred yards from the edge of the village. She knew if they passed close to one of the homes, somebody would be obliged to ask them in. They would take off their shoes and use the outhouse. The intimacy of the thought scared her silly.

Hospitality was the problem. Mother knew a hostess in Mongolia must be ready to serve tea, sourdough bread, and jam at a moment's notice. If company stayed more than forty-five minutes, the hostess must start the soup. Her mouth watered just thinking about it: chunks of mutton, thick noodles, carrots, cabbage and rutabaga. Indeed, if they were invited in they would be devouring that family's winter rations, and she would disappear the next day without a chance to reciprocate.

She dug her feet stubbornly in the snow and would go no further.

New to the rules of Mongolian hospitality, she didn't know their visit would mean a year of good luck for the family, *the good luck of a hundred horses* –prosperity.

Mother came from a land where the rules were upside down, where you apologized for arriving during mealtime, where you sent children home to be fed by their own mothers.

"Come on, let's go," Father called. "It'll be okay."

"I don't know why, but I can't," Mother replied.

Someday she would learn that in this land, the dining table is set after the guests arrived, and the rituals before supper include the guests. The ancient blood of supreme hospitality ran through the veins and warmed the heart of the countryside Mongolians.

While the children walked on ahead, Father implored mother one more time. "Come on, let's visit."

"You know they will serve milk tea, and how the children will refuse it," was Mother's last excuse.

The wind swirled about them. The family was somber as they trudged through the snow back to the cold resort and drank hot cups of water in silence before crashing for the night.

Around midnight, a party of young people in the adjacent

room danced to disco music into the early morning hours. The noise reached fever pitch as the youth jumped from bed to bed and vodka bottles crashed to the floor.

In Search of Light

Ulaanbaatar
December 1996

Dressed in layers for Siberian wind, stuffed into a narrow seat near the back, I watch out the window for my stop. The trolley wheels rattle beneath my boots, clicking off the blocks as I venture farther than I would normally go on my own.

This unfamiliar territory lies west of the 3rd and 4th District by way of the Big Ring Road—where it drops south to a major intersection. There, the Hanamasa Restaurant sits next to a large bus stop and a proliferation of new shops, one of which, I hope, carries Christmas lights.

The clouds hang as low as my spirits. I admit that I need the lights as much as the children. Even in my dreams, I find myself groping around in shadowy interiors for the light switch.

"Don't you just love it here?" The question has haunted me ever since that American lady with the tasteful makeup and glossy fingernails asked it. That's an easy question to ask in the middle of summer when everything is green and the sky is crystal blue and the air is pure and a glass of water doesn't freeze on the kitchen counter.

To be truthful, my days are full of language learning and frustration. We have been here in Mongolia for a full year and a half. *Count the months.* Eighteen, and I still don't understand what people are saying to me. How many different ways are there to ask me where I'm from?

I don't know if it's my tutor or just the nature of our relationship, but I feel like Eliza Doolittle who was condemned for "the cold-blooded murder of the English tongue." Professor Higgins found her on the dirty streets of London and forced her into a linguistic make-over. Like her, I must conquer pure vowels. Only in the movie, the characters break out into song, and here we march through the streets in a gray fog and spend half the day looking for just one thing.

I see the Hanamasa. It's time to get off. I stand near a group

of shoppers and commuters at the back of the trolley to the screech of the brakes and the scraping call of the metal spring that rides the electric line above me.

Which one of us will be the first out the door? *Let's race.*

I look around, but there's no sign of the shops others have told me about. Looks to me like there are mostly food markets. Through the tunnel entrance and under the low hanging ceilings, I search all the isles, but there's nothing here but what I can find in every other shop: vegetables, bread, packaged instant coffee, waffle cookies and Russian layered cake with its lard for frosting.

Out in the open, I see apartment buildings and an auto body repair, but nothing that can pass for a store. I decide to wait for a bus that will take me to the Russian District on the east side. Push that man out of my way, squeeze past the older women, and find a place to sit.

This is where the main character—that would be me— should stand and sing, *with a little bit, with a little bit, with a little bit of luck we'll find some lights! With a little bit...*

Oh, yeah. I better watch my bag. Everything bad that has happened to me has happened on a bus. There was the mugging, and the time my friend Diane was nearly trampled. She'd gone out of her way to give me a tour of the food shops and look what happened to her. She popped off the bus like a cork from a bottle of fermenting brew, and not a soul helped her up from the pavement. Tall and lovely Dianne, dusting herself off before I could reach her!

I've stopped singing.

Brave woman, I will be like you. I will live above my circumstances, learn to laugh at myself and learn how to sing on gray days. Help me, Jesus.

Giving up on the lights is not an option. The Russian district comes into view with its four-story apartments and playgrounds swept clean. However, the man who sits beside me is apparently drunk and has such a firm grip on the seat in front of us that I can't get out.

I shake his shoulder and call him, "Akhaa." Though he's not my older brother, he's due respect whether he's stone drunk or not. He releases his grip on the seat, but his torso slumps lower until his arm wraps around my leg. I look up with pleading eyes to the bus conductor, the woman with the money bag strapped over her shoulder, and she pulls at the man until he stumbles into the aisle so I can leave.

This area is a little more familiar. I've been to the Russian school and to the hospital which houses a restaurant on the back that uses the blue and white table service. I've only been there once. The stuffed cabbage rolls with sour cream were amazing. *I wonder where they buy the sour cream?*

The soundtrack of my life picks up where I left off. *With a little bit, with a little bit...*

I spot a door with a sign that says магазин, mah-ga-zeen, in stenciled letters. That means *store* in Russian. Nearly frozen to the bone and hands too stiff to manage the door knob, I'm thankful another customer is on her way out. I step into a room of no more than four meters squared. *Oh, my. They have yellow split peas. I didn't*

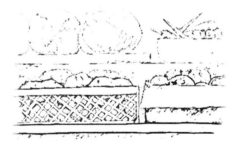 *know there was such a thing.* I think I'm smiling. Songs are in my head again. Split pea soup. *Now wouldn't that be luverly?*

I wonder how different I will be when the transformation is complete, I mean, when I can truly speak Mongolian? *Will I be good for anything else?* Eliza asked the same question. Maybe she would've been happier left where she was.

Glass half full or half empty?

Look on the upside, you have a kilo of split peas in your bag.

One more bus stop, and I will be home. I stomp my feet to keep warm.

That's strange. The vehicle that pulls up along the curb is nearly empty. It's just me and the conductor. I hand her fifty *tughrik*, and she gives me the meaningless slip of paper--proof that I've paid the fare, though there are a thousand littered beneath our feet and no one else around. She's trying to talk to me, but I can't understand her.

"Would you say that again more slowly?" I say in Mongolian.

"Something, something, *drooga*," she says.

Drugs. She wants to sell me drugs! Mission training didn't prepare me for this. I'll turn her down politely and change my seat to the back, but she follows me. "Something, something, *drooga*" she says again.

Perhaps she's not using Mongolian at all, but rather Russian. I guess I could look Russian to her, especially if I'm not smiling.

Smile. You're a happy Christian woman with a song in your heart.

She asks about the drugs again. I look away. Smiling isn't helping.

My last steps home are labored. I've been out for hours, and all I have to show for it is some shortbread cookies and split peas.

When I get to the top of the stairs, I note our apartment door has been left open a crack. We never leave our doors unlocked.

"Hello!" I call out, pushing the door wide. "Anyone there?"

The corridor is quiet, so I turn toward the living room and hear shouts of "Merry Christmas" and "Surprise!" My husband and children jump up from the couch, and Mary the youngest screams with delight, "Look!"

Above me, a long string of brightly covered lights encircles the room near the ceiling and finishes with a grand finale, a little Christmas tree with several small gifts wrapped beneath it.

"Joanna and I went shopping too!" Pete yells.

In this world, there is light. There is Dianne, and my family, and songs.

Before bed, I search through the dictionary until I find the word I'm looking for. There in the pages marked with a ᴀ, I find that in Russian the word Друг [droog] —means *friend*.

Looking Back

A few miles north of Ulaanbaatar
September 1996
References to the cities of Darkhan and Erdenet
May 1993

The doors of the all the yurts open toward the Bogd Khan Mountain. From a distance, the mountain appears bald, however, aspen and tamarack line its valleys. The Tuul River travels along the bold edges of this sacred national forest like a ribbon of dark blue. North of the city, the hillsides are dotted with summer cabins, which range in quality from shacks to elaborate summer cottages.

A spring bubbles up out of the ground near the front door of the summer house owned by the parents of my language helper Naraa. Our hosts are preparing Mongolian-style barbecue for our family of five and my father visiting from the States. I'm not sure of their names, but as culture dictates, we call them Grandmother and Grandfather, and all the family members by their rank: older brother, younger brother, older sister, and so forth.

My family and I follow Naraa's husband along the gurgling stream. Up ahead, it will join a wider tributary to feed the Tuul River before it leaves the city on the west side to skirt past the airport.

"Look for large, smooth stones," Naraa's husband calls.

I swish my hand around in the cold water and choose an oblong stone, somewhat blue in color, larger than my palm, its sharp edges washed away by the perpetual movement of the water. I hear happy shouts from the girls and watch Pete tuck a stone in the pocket of his hoodie.

I muse on how far we've come in the adjustment process. Part of our success has been making opportunities to get out and enjoy nature. It seems like we're drawn to the river again and again.

With my hand in the cold stream, I am taken back to our first visit to the steppes of Mongolia in May of 1993. Bill and I left our children with my family in South Dakota while we toured the cities of Ulaanbaatar, Darkhan and Erdenet.

Evidently the only travelers out on the road, the driver parked the antiquated Russian limousine on the highway, and Bill and I crunched over the glistening snow to the edge of a river. Large fragments of ice floated past, and the blue sky stretched wide and clear in the sun—so much so—that the bright snow hurt my eyes.

Our translator was a man of 35 years old, a new Christian and possible informant for the government. We had to trust him, as he was assigned to us by those who prepared our visas and travel papers. Any new convert to Christianity might be an infiltration on the part of the old order, the Mongolian version of the KGB.

The thought of someone spying on us and our friends left a foreign taste in my mouth. Yet, through him we interpreted the world around us and everything spoken.

The driver felt our journey was remarkable. He called it charmed or blessed—his reasons: we left the city in one piece, had no car troubles, had a good night's sleep in a decent hotel, and experienced no harassment for looking like Russians.

The city square of Darkhan City was close to our hotel, and though the Iron Curtain had come down, twenty-foot tall propaganda banners still waved in the wind from the stately structures that surrounded the plaza, all a tangible reminder of the nation's recent past.

In the first years of the transition, I doubt the average family like Naraa's could have relaxed like they are today. Unemployment was the norm and most days were spent in long lines for bread and other staples with the family's ration card clutched tightly.

Naraa calls us back to assemble our stones in a pile on the campfire. Only a few are culled out and thrown back into the stream.

At the door of the cabin, the grandmother motions for Naraa and I to help in the kitchen. The natural light from the small window over the well-worn counter top will be adequate enough to peel and chop a mountain of vegetables.

Grandmother sits on a traditional low stool with a bucket between her legs, an ingenious way for catching the potato peelings. She wears her countryside housecoat, ratty and torn at the edges, grease stains on the chest. She points me toward the carrots and onions. I enjoy the work, my head in a cloud of first impressions of the nation.

Back in 1993, the restaurant in Erdenet City served thinly-sliced cucumber and shaves of beef tongue arranged artistically on the plate. I told my stomach it was all I needed, hoping soup would arrive shortly. I felt like I was hungry every minute since I had gotten off the plane. Hot broth would fill me, I mean, fool me for an hour or two.

At that meal, we met the famous Swedish missionaries. It was easy to see why all the newcomers from the States were jealous of them. They lived among the people and "If you closed your eyes when the husband spoke," the locals said, "you would think he was a *jinken Mongol*."

Sitting in that fancy restaurant with the glassy tabletop and linen napkins and savoring my last slice of cucumber, I wondered if we would be good missionaries. Could we really bring our children to this place? Every store I entered had bare shelves. On my day to tour the market, there was only tea, rice, ketchup, cabbage and scouring powder. Bread lines for those with ration cards lined the courtyard of the shopping area of San Sar.

With no agenda after meeting the Swedish couple, we turned back toward the capital in search of a town to show the *Jesus Film*.

An hour down the bumpy road, we pulled into a little village through a tall city gate of bright blue. The name is lost to me now, but it seemed like all the vehicles of the entire village were parked in a single row in front of a two-story building. I was soon to discover it was the school –kindergarten on the first floor, older grades on the second.

My husband Bill and the translator entered the building to ask if this would be a good evening to show the *Jesus Film*. "Would the villagers like to learn about the founder of the Christian faith?"

I cringed with the fear of rejection and that awkward sense of being the outsider, the proselytizer. However, my misgivings were waylaid when the head schoolmaster said he was thrilled at the honor of foreign guests for Graduation Day.

Girls giggled, running past us in their brown uniform dresses with white ruffled pinafores. A circus of white anklet socks and black patent leather shoes marched to the second floor. There would be guests and a movie!

"Won't you sit at the table of honor and enjoy the feast?" the translator spoke for the mayor.

Nondescript bottles of orange soda appeared before us, vodka for the men, and milk tea in blue and white porcelain cups. Dried yoghurt treats called *aaruul* rested in bowls with chocolates wrapped in bright red and blue cellophane.

Then came the unsweetened yoghurt. An older woman in a cotton apron handed me a bowl, frothy and full up to the brim.

"Drink!" said the translator.

I put the bowl to my lips, and felt the zing of the live-culture. For every swallow I managed, the yoghurt reproduced itself in my bowl. My insides were alive with activity. Who would save me?

Soon the graduates, sparkly-eyed and eager, pulled on our arms to follow them to the top floor where dancing was underway. Thanks to their prodding, Bill and I danced to Abba's *Dancing Queen* under the disco ball spinning from the ceiling.

I laugh out loud at the thought of Bill and I bouncing side by side with the Mongolian teenagers.

My mountain of carrots is nearly all chopped.

"What's so funny?" Bill asks, ducking his head to enter the summer house. He squints adjusting to the lack of light.

"Oh, nothing. Is the meat ready?" I reply.

"The goat's been slaughtered, skinned, and butchered. We're waiting on you."

"We'll be right there," I say, and turn to help with the potatoes.

Parents, grandparents and children stuffed themselves into the largest classroom on the top floor of the school. You could have heard a pin drop through most of the movie as the book of Luke unfolded the history of Jesus' teaching and miracles.

The sense of uneasiness returned to my stomach. It wasn't the meal, nor could I blame it on the yoghurt. When the Roman soldiers pounded the nails into Jesus' wrists, the girls sobbed and their shoulders heaved. They had no idea that was coming.

After the showing, one man took us aside and asked through our translator if it was fair for God to wait until the end of the 20th century to share the story of his son. Shouldn't they have had a timelier opportunity?

We didn't have an answer.

Naraa calls us to carry the vegetables out to the campfire, and I shake off the past.

"You don't want to miss this. My brother is going to fill the milk can."

The first signs of dusk appear in the sky with a wide band of pale pink. The men throw chunks of goat meat—bones and all—into the metal, pressurized milk can. Then they take long, handmade tongs and layer the meat with the hot river rocks taken from the fire.

Next come the onions, potatoes, rutabaga, and carrots. Naraa pours in a liter of water, and her mother adds small handfuls of salt, saving some to throw over her shoulder. The brother clamps down the lid and nestles the can into the hot coals to pressure cook.

"Now we wait," Naraa says.

We squat on our haunches near the fire to stay warm while the meat and vegetables cook. In this place where quiet is revered, I return to my memories.

It was time to leave the little village for the capital, and the mayor met us outside the school. "Do you have any materials to hand out?" he asked.

"We have copies of the book of Luke translated into Mongolian," the translator replied.

"Well, if you are going to hand them out, it must be fair. Do you have enough copies for everyone?" the mayor asked.

"I believe we do. At least for all of the adults."

The box of books was located in the back of the car, and the mayor took them in his arms.

"Now this is unusual! The people will likely read them if the mayor hands them out," the translator whispered.

We watched the mayor proceed to the river's edge to hand out the books to the older women resting on benches. Then, a young woman in her twenties approached us from the side of the school.

We learned her story. When she was at the Great University in Ulaanbaatar, she became acquainted with the teachings of Christ and became one of his followers. But having returned to her hometown to work, she had been worried about how to survive as a Christian without support. So far, when she brought up the topic of Jesus Christ, no one understood who she was talking about. But now, nearly everyone had seen the movie and they all had a copy of the gospel in their hands. Now she could say, "Have you read it? Do you want to read with me?"

As far as she was concerned, our visit was a sign of God's love for her.

The campfire crackles and snaps. The milk can whistles wildly. "Is it ready yet?" Naraa's son calls out from wandering along the river with our children.

Naraa's husband drags the can from the fire to let it cool a bit and to check the contents. He lifts the clamp and the lid flies back. Steam rises with the delightful smell of the meat mingled with onions and vegetables. The faces of our hosts glow in the light of the fire, no doubt as excited to share the meal as we are to receive.

I turn toward the summer house and follow Naraa for the utensils and plates. The sun is setting behind the summer house with a wild fury of pink, purple, and orange.

"Now we will pass the rocks, hot from the inside of the milk can," Naraa's husband explains.

A river rock lands in my hands like a game of hot potato. I toss it back and forth from my right hand to my left and back again. "Tell me the history of this tradition," I say, passing on the hot stone to my daughter next to me.

"Perhaps, the ancient warriors did this to warm their hands on long, cold journeys," Naraa replies.

"Sure makes for good circulation," her husband says smiling.

Next comes the best of the broth from the bottom of the milk can. We each take a sip from the community bowl. The oil burns at the bottom of my empty belly.

The sun sets behind our host, a hot line of red along the horizon. Dusk has fully descended. Everyone talks at the same time, excitement mounting as Naraa's mother removes all the steamed vegetables in a bowl and her father reaches in for the meat.

The men's pocket knives suddenly appear, and the women receive the more succulent pieces. To express our contentment, we smack our lips.

"Have you ever seen the *Jesus Film?*" Bill asks Naraa's husband.

On the way home in the taxicab, our family of five rides in silence. The stars are out. The beauty of this moment is an echo of our first visit to the countryside. A few miles from home, the joyful refrain sung by the new Mongolian believers runs through my head, "From the rising of the sun to its setting, the name of the Lord be praised."

Giving Haircuts by Candlelight

Joanna at home in Gants Hudag (One Well)
Northeastern corner of Ulaanbaatar
Late 1997 or 1998

It's Friday evening. Dad's driving us home from school in the company van. Things are tense. He needs to squeeze us through a congested area where shoppers board the trolleys and where four lanes merge into one big mess. Most of the trucks are headed for the material supply district called *Zuun Ail*. That's Mongolian for *One Hundred Neighbors*. Once I went there with my father when we were building our new house. I remember a twisting road with dozens of little shops on each side. Every shop exploded with boxes of greasy nails and pipe fittings, and I had to watch my step because there were piles of lumber and stacks of glass everywhere. In some shops the men flirted with me. They talked about my eyes and my blonde hair. That made me pretty uncomfortable, so I pretended I didn't understand.

The van struggles to make it to the top of the washed-out gravel road. It happens to be the closest entrance to our subdivision. On either side are yurts of dirty wool, wooden shacks, a couple of log cabins, and plenty of wild dogs. Up ahead, an elderly man in a dusty old Mongol dress is pulling a large, aluminum milk container in a rickety cart. I know he's bringing water for his family from the spring near the marshes. Dad doesn't see him at first. Now he does.

To avoid hitting him, Dad jerks the van quickly to the right. From my window, I see the man lose his balance. The cart flips on its side, and the water spills down the hill. I've watched that man pull his water past our fence a hundred times over. But this is the first time I see him.

"Dad, stop!" I yell from my seat in the back. "Let's help him!"

Dad doesn't seem to hear me. I crane my neck to catch a final glimpse of the man. He's picking up the can and setting it back on the cart. A strange feeling catches in my throat.

The van comes to a lurching stop at the gate of our *khashaa*. There's no word like it in English. I think it means something halfway between *yard* and *fence*. Really, our yard is a courtyard of dust. To the left stands the house, to the right the coal shed and horse shelter. Oh, the outhouse is close to the gate. We can't forget the outhouse. Mom painted it bright blue. In fact, she added the paint to the eaves of the buildings, to the front door of our house, and to every wooden surface she could find. She thinks our *khashaa* looks so much better. Personally, I think her efforts are useless. But at least she tries.

Dad beeps the horn and pops out of the truck to open the gate. Soon we pull through the humble archway to park beside our humble home of straw bales and plaster. We run from the van. After our chores are done, we can watch videos or ride the horses up to the meadows. Although, I don't think we will today since it's my brother Pete's turn to help the house helper Anna with dinner. My sister Mary will filter water for me because I've been recruited to cut hair.

"Joanna! Lynn's here with the girls. They're ready for haircuts!" Mom yells from the front door.

She's waving that plastic salon cape around. I think about how many times she's mentioned how glad she is that she brought that thing from the States.

After a quick snack of hard peanuts covered in candied yoghurt, I pick up the scissors. Mom sits with the cape fastened around her neck. She chats freely with Lynn. I pull on a section of hair with the comb and snip.

Mary rushes through the chores to meet Lynn's younger girls who are playing outside with the dogs. She slips on her play boots and dashes out the front. The door slams behind her. Sparky our Jack Russell terrier is hilarious to watch. He knows how to outwit the other two dogs in games of chase. His favorite place to run is behind the outhouse where he turns back the way he came. It fools Fudge and Budge every time.

"Hold still," I say firmly. "I'm going to cut the back first, then the sides, and then the top."

"Can you believe we're trusting a twelve-year old to do our

hair?" Mom says turning her head toward Lynn, waiting for her turn in the chair.

"My last haircut turned out great. And who can beat the price?" Lynn teases.

"Getting paid would be nice," I say, centering my mother's chin again. I take another snip.

"Oh, there's no problem trusting her with scissors. Joanna has magic hands. Remember how she gave the penicillin to the horses?"

"I thought you were the one giving the shots."

"Well, I gave the first round, but I did something wrong and the horse collapsed on the ground."

"You sent the medicine straight into its bloodstream! You're supposed to get it into the muscle," I add.

"Like I said, she has magic hands," Mom says.

"You should be a doctor when you grow up," Lynn offers.

I raise my eyebrows. I can't say I've never thought about it.

Pete is squeezing the Polish-style ketchup into the bubbling pot of meat and fried vegetables. "Not all of it!" I hear Anna say.

Suddenly, a loud motor rumbles in the yard outside our front door. I think about putting down the scissors to find out what's going on. Then, there's a scream. We bolt for the front door to see what's happening, and we're met by the young girls in distress. Mary is holding her forearm.

Behind them, a man on a motorcycle takes off his helmet.

"Mine," he says in Mongolian which might mean he is taking the blame, though Mongols seem to experience a lot of trouble with that concept. "The big black dog startled and turned to bite. He caught the girl."

We look to Mary, "When I pulled back my arm, his teeth ripped a hole in me." She pulled back the sleeve of her sweatshirt with one hand.

We stare in disbelief. She continues in the matter-of-fact tone of the Mongolians, "Look, no blood."

I inspect her skin. There is a gaping wound —an inch deep and two inches long. It's a clean cut as if it had been done with a knife. The women watch over my shoulder and pull back in alarm. Dad joins us from tending the van which gets parked at the neighbor's.

"What's going on?" he asks.

With explanation complete, Dad concedes that she needs stitches. The cyclist turns his bike around in a cloud of dust, leaving us clueless to the reason for his coming in the first place.

"The only doctor that I know who might help us is the German doctor. I'll call," Dad says.

The motorbike rumbles in the distance.

"I want to go with you," I say and escort Mary into the house. She's still calm, looking up to me for our next step. "Let's run alcohol over this before we go, and I'll bandage it tight."

Back in the van, we descend the gravel road cautiously.

Perhaps Dad is more aware that this path is for locals, or maybe he's concerned with Mary's comfort. In either case, he takes a more conservative speed, and we proceed to the heart of the city.

We don't have the apartment number for the doctor, but we know the building where most Germans live. So, Dad parks the vehicle in an open spot on the street and calls the doctor on the cell phone again. "Dr. Friedman?"*

Mary and I stand close. I look over my shoulder. Behind the three of us, the sun is going down with an intense, red glow. I turn back. Before us, the windows of the apartments are ablaze with yellow light. I hear the doctor's voice, "You've caught me during my wedding reception, so I'll come out. We'll go over to the clinic together."

*not the doctor's real name

While we wait with our bodies resting against the van, I think about which is more amazing: that the doctor will leave his wedding party or that he is here in Mongolia in the first place.

In the first three years we lived here, I'm not sure there was a single doctor in the whole city that spoke English or had been trained in the West.

A tall man in new jeans and a dress shirt comes out of the building and walks towards us. We step towards him. He greets us.

"Call me Dr. Fred." The doctor extends his hand. Dr. Fred has a trim haircut and has such a pleasant, sincere smile. We climb into his black Mercedes, and he works the streets to his clinic.

From my seat in the back, I lean forward to ask him questions. "How long have you worked in Mongolia?" "Where did you work before?"

Dr. Fred answers cheerfully. He describes the village in Kenya where he worked before he came here. He tells us about an emergency surgery he performed on a boy who fell out of a window. "In the States, I'd never be allowed to do such a thing. But when you're in the Third World...there's no one to say anything about it."

The conversation continues as we enter the courtyard of the Embassy. A few trees that line the sidewalk block the light of the moon. There are no street lights, so it's dark. Birds call goodnight. The earth turns a bit. Or maybe it's the moon that moves, so that the white of the moon shines on the door of the clinic where Dr. Fred works the key.

I realize I've been ignoring my patient. I step away from the men to squeeze Mary's hand.

Dr. Fred lifts Mary up onto the operating table. He talks with Mary about the wound with optimism. "It's a clean wound. Your sweatshirt didn't rip which means the dog's saliva never made contact. Lucky for you."

To me, "Will you be our nurse? Here, hold this."

I hold the packet of sterilized needles and topical anesthetic. He even lets me apply the iodine before the procedure! I look up for approval. He nods his head. Mary squeezes her eyes shut.

Much too soon, our visit to the clinic is over and we take the moonlit drive back to the van to say our goodbyes. We smother the doctor with profuse *thank you's* and promises to send gifts since he has refused our money. The doctor walks away, and Mary says, "He's nice."

I do not answer her. I can't speak. The rush I felt at the clinic has left me, but the desire to be a doctor burns like the hot, red coals of our wood-stove. We pass a hundred homes now, two hundred even! The marsh sparkles in the light of the moon. The river winds between the two valleys. Large rocks that line the river sit in their familiar places, so majestic in the moonlight.

I lean towards my father, "Dad, take the long way."

He smiles.

We proceed past the rocky entrance to our subdivision, and I see that the electricity is out in our neighborhood. We pass the bus stop with its kiosks, closed for the night. We turn at the corner where Dad found the orphaned kitten. Most homes are completely dark. Just the stars twinkle above us.

Now I see candles in the windows of the corner store. I wave to the woman walking with her two children. I imagine they will buy sausage and a kilogram of rice. We're getting close now. The women are waiting for their haircuts.

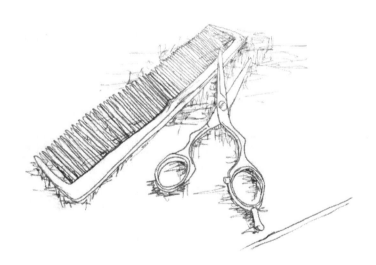

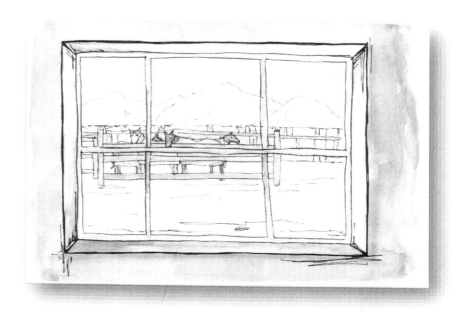

Where Fahrenheit Meets Celsius

At home at Gants Hudag (One Well)
Northeast corner of Ulaanbaatar
January 1998

The day begins with hot tea, not the salty milk tea of my neighbors, but rather the standard black. I step away from the kitchen to sit on a stool next to the wood-stove in the center of our home, slurping loudly, drawing the tea through my lips.

I think about women in shacks and yurts throughout the

nation who must prioritize keeping their homes warm today. Heat sources are dwindling; the city coalbin is nearly empty. Even our kindling is a humble pile outside the front door, left-overs from the construction of our "straw bale home."

I set the mug down to stoke the fire, fighting the length of the sticks. When the fire crescendos with a chorus of crackle and hiss, I turn the damper to the left. The clay wall behind the stove is giving off a measure of heat, but even our eighteen-inch-thick walls are no rival for the January wind which sweeps past the prison, circles the district called "One Well," and beats hard against our edges.

I pick up my tea again and gulp down its hot, sugary goodness, hoping the fire will not go out on my watch. I look out the front window which frames our five Mongolian horses, gifts to our children to ease the guilt for taking them half-way across the world. Their stocky bodies are covered in hoary ice from head to foot with only a circle of color around their nostrils, revealing their coats of black, chestnut, and bay. The horses, motionless and regal, face the rolling hills to the distant west and watch for the return of summer's green and crystal blue.

"Hang in there, Chocolate," I whisper to the yearling, the youngest of our horses, as if he can hear me. He wears a thick wool blanket like a shield from the frigid temperature. Earlier at breakfast, my husband announced to the family that it reached forty-below-zero last night, the place where Celsius and Fahrenheit meet.

"It's the coldest we'll see it," he said, "...it's awful hard on Chocolate. He should've eaten twice as much as the others."

This morning before the sun pushed through the thick clouds of a thousand coal fires, my husband went out to the garage to start the van. By placing an electric coil under the oil pan to thin out the sludge, he keeps the oil thin enough to circulate like blood through our bodies.

Mary our youngest returned from her outdoor chores and announced, "My horse is dying."

"Don't worry, honey. I'll find us a vet," I promised.

Before Mary left with her siblings for school, she lingered at the fence of the corral and looked back at me with sober green eyes.

Now, an hour later, I wonder how I will find a veterinarian without a phonebook, without letting the house get cold, and how do you say "veterinarian" in Mongolian?

Thankfully, my language tutor is coming. Her name is Bor which simply means *Brown*. She will arrive in a wool coat that comes to her knees. Beneath her coat will be a wool skirt, layers of sweaters and a cashmere vest. Skillfully, she will wrap two scarves around her head and neck. Without these, the cold air will feel like a million knives. Over several pairs of socks and undergarments, she'll put on the ever-popular Russian leather boots, and even though they are impractical, she will make the trek on their narrow heels. Cold days are no excuse for not meeting regularly. Every day is cold.

I decide to make her favorite apple cake and will insist she take it to her family. I imagine her cherry-like cheeks pushing her eyes up into half-moons.

As our lesson begins, we both have something on our minds. I need to know how to find a veterinarian, but Bor is refusing to speak to me anymore. Have I heard her correctly?

"Your consonants are so sharp that they hurt my ears, with your t's and k's and g's. Today you will soften everything. You've heard drunken men on the trolleys. Talk like them."

She wants me to change the way I speak Mongolian right this very minute.

"Read this paragraph, not so *ha-tuu*," she says.

The English equivalent for *ha-tuu* is *hard* or *harsh*, and it's one of a handful of words that sound remotely like their English equivalent. There is the word *eet* for eat and *nudeskin* for naked, and I would be hard pressed to think of another one.

She drills me on softer articulation, and I promise to

remember this new way of speaking at all times. She's pleased and folds her hands and says our lesson is complete. So, I serve up hot tea and apple cake, and we stare out the window at the horses. Tsagaa our horse wrangler has arrived and will take them down to the spring for water. Bor and I watch from the window as he gathers the herd. He opens the gate, but Chocolate will not move. Instead, he crumples to the ground on his hind legs. Tsagaa pulls at his mouth to put on his harness, but the poor horse clenches his teeth.

Tsagaa enters the house and stops on the special rug designated for standing and talking indoors with your boots on. He will give me a report, but I know what he will say before he says it. If Chocolate stays on the ground, he will never get back up again.

"Here are five-thousand *tughrik* to find a veterinarian for me," I beg, trying to speak with softness.

"It's too late for a doctor. When I come back from the spring, I'll try to work with him. But you could give him another bottle of that fennel tea."

He lumbers out the door with the harness still in hand, his head uncovered, his boots too big for him, his sweater and coat too thin.

I turn to Bor. "Can you help me with the horse before you go?"

We brew up the fennel tea and offer it to the suffering horse.

After half a liter, he repositions himself. Even with my *ha-tuu* Mongolian, he will not get up, not with all the coaxing in the world.

My tutor motions that it's time to leave, so I walk her to the bus stop, arm in arm as Mongolians do, and I reflect upon this custom. It is more than just enjoying the warmth of another human being. When I'm close to Bor, I'm adopted into the Mongol race. Her bloodline flows through me, and I think about how Mongols survive cold winters.

I stoke the fire and make another cup of tea to warm myself. But when I try to fill the large kettle for soup, the water comes out of the spigot in slow drips. The car battery that forces water from the tank to the sink is working but the pipes are frozen.

I should call my husband. Frozen pipes are reason enough to call him home from work, and I'll ask him to take the children out of school early. I want them to be here when Chocolate passes away.

The house bursts with excitement upon their return. My husband brings Sukhbaatar with him. He's the oldest in his family, playing the role of father and breadwinner for several sisters. His family is forever entwined with ours—with history of holidays spent together, employment, and loans. He enters with the others looking eager to be useful.

Pete and Joanna, our older children are convinced they can save the poor horse. So, they locate blankets to cover him, and they force the last half of the tea down his throat. Meanwhile, my husband discusses our situation with Sukhbaatar in the room that stores our massive water tank, a castoff from a dairy farm.

My husband finds me. "I'll bring in some coal. After that, I will go for the vet. In the meantime, do whatever Sukhbaatar tells you to do. Chocolate will hang on a few more hours."

I stoke the fire.

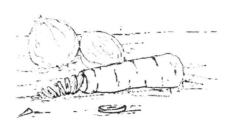 Sukhbaatar has not called for me yet, so I start to chop onions, to peel and dice carrots. Sukhbaatar's sister Sara arrives to help me with the noon meal. She cuts and pulls the beef into little chunks and fries them in the wok on the stove. Aromas of meat and onion fill our home.

But we hear a shout for help from the water room. Sukhbaatar pokes his head out with a terrified look on his face.

"What is it?" I come running.

"Go and get Bill before he leaves!" His tone is throaty and harsh.

I catch Bill going through the gate, and he abandons the vehicle. The children follow him into the house, all except Mary who has sat down on the frozen ground next to Chocolate to begin her vigil.

"Sukhbaatar's caught our house on fire!" Bill is using a voice he has never used before. "He used a blowtorch and a stray piece of straw caught fire. Pete! Get an ax!"

I don't know what to do first. We will need more than water to stop our house from burning to the ground. Joanna our twelve-year old has climbed down into the tank of freezing water and hands up a bucket to her father. Her older brother Pete climbs on the roof with an ax.

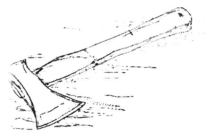

"Gouge a hole right above me!" Bill shouts but no one can hear him outside. So, I run out the front and instructions to Pete. His first attempts are timid. How strange to destroy the house you just finished building with your father!

I know we need more buckets, so I cross our yard to the next, forcing Sara to go with me. I have to use my *ha-tuu* voice.

"The big black dog," she cries.

It's true that the neighbor's dog is larger than any other dog in the whole country, a wolfhound, a monster, but I say, "My house is on fire and you're worried about a dog?"

As we pass through the gate to my neighbor's yard, time slows. I look back to see Sara following on my heels, her face full of fear. I know Mary is with her horse. I know Pete is on the roof. I know Sukhbaatar and Bill are pulling up buckets of water from

Joanna who stands knee deep.

I must do something to keep my family here in this formidable country. I recall the first winter in Mongolia when we lived in a high-rise apartment downtown. Even with semi-modern conveniences there were challenges. I wondered if I would have the toughness, the resolve to stick it out. Just locating a bag of rice and a head of cabbage could take hours. One day in January, as cold as this one, I looked out the kitchen window at the smoky skies and icy streets. I thought, *If I don't get out in that cold and hunt through that market, there will be nothing to eat for dinner.*

That strength is still inside me. I march to the neighbors, a bulldog that won't let go.

In the next beat, I yell out in English, not caring who hears me, "If our house burns down, I'm leaving!"

The next hour is a blur of buckets and bodies, a swarm of neighbors, Tsagaa, Sara, Sukhbaatar, me and the children—all putting out the fire.

Only Mary is absent. The late afternoon sun casts her shadow across the body of her dying horse.

We save the house.

We sit down together in the living room for a plateful of dry noodles tossed with slivers of tasty beef and fried vegetables. When Pete says to pass the ketchup, he looks up at the wide and gaping hole to the cold, dark sky above his bedroom.

The next morning everyone stays home.

I motion for Mary to sit with me by the wood-stove. I will hold back the information I have. Though Mary can talk circles around us in the local language and scare off wild dogs with rocks, she wouldn't understand her horse given away as meat for the poor. Instead, we talk about how sweet Chocolate was and describe their lovely rides across the open steppes.

"When people die, they lay them out on the top of the mountain for the birds," she says.

"Sukhbaatar will take care of things," I say.

"He was a good horse," Mary replies.

"You were a faithful friend, right to the very end." I drop a big spoonful of sugar into her tea.

She nods her head and reaches for the drink.

"I'm sorry we couldn't do both," my voice comes in broken pieces. "With everyone helping on the house, there was no one to go for the vet."

"I know," she says managing a smile.

We huddle together in front of the wood-stove with our mugs of tea. We are side by side, so close that our arms touch.

Pushing Uphill

The Bubbling Springs Work Center (Orgilokh Bolag)
13ᵗʰ Micro-district, Bayanzurkh, Ulaanbaatar
1998

LORI: Before everyone goes their own way, I
           want to read the story I wrote
           about Grandpa's trip to Mongolia.

PETE: *(flopping down on the sofa)*
           Which one?

LORI: It was his third one, in 1998.

JOANNA: Okay, just give us a minute to get settled. *(Joanna and Mary crowd onto the sofa next to their brother)*

BILL: This better be good. *(choosing his favorite chair)*

LORI: Is everybody ready? If you hear something that doesn't sound right, be sure to correct me.

In front of the airport, standing in the brisk, cold air of Mongolian autumn, the driver of an old Mercedes Benz agreed to take Grandpa Jim and his traveling companion Dave to the construction site in the center of the city, where they would join a work team from Washington state. Along with the assistance of a small Mongolian crew, the men planned to frame the upper stories of a multipurpose complex—12,000 square feet—dedicated to office space, meeting rooms, and micro-business incubation.

Proceeding toward the city, on their right, the foothills of the Bogd Khan Mountains took shape like a giant lying down for a rest, and the narrow highway slid along the edge of its ankles, knees, and elbow.

"Up here, before we turn off toward the city itself, you'll see where my grandchildren and I took a long walk up there two years ago and had a picnic in the tamarack and the aspen. The leaves turn yellow, just like back in Colorado."

The taxi entered the edge of the city now and the bus stop

shelters for those who must wait in the cold clicked past their vehicle on the right. Near each bus stop was a kiosk, little buildings made of metal with a door on the side or the back and a front window that slid open for the vendor to sell snacks, sodas, and cigarettes.

"That place is selling cucumbers, and I think I saw a sign for Snickers®, so I guess we won't starve," Dave announced.

PETE: *Most people called the kiosks, "toots." Why don't you use that name?*

LORI: No one would recognize it, and then I'd have to explain.

PETE: The toots are one of my favorite things about Mongolia. No matter where you are in the city, you can just walk a little distance and you'll find one, see if there's something you want to buy, and it's yours. I had no trouble learning the numbers, that way I could ask how much everything cost.

LORI: Back to the story?

"Don't worry," Jim replied, "Lori will make sure there's a cook for all the workers on the building. They'll mostly make American food. That way we won't have troubles with our digestion and can work at our optimum. We only have eight days."

At this, the taxi began to chug and spurt and came to a grinding halt on the side of the road.

Jim leaned over in Dave's direction, "I think we'll have to get out and push."

"What! You're serious?"

"It's just to that gas station over there," Jim replied, his hand on the door handle, his head motioning to a small building painted bright blue about 200 yards ahead. "See it?"

The driver put the transmission into neutral and got out to steer the vehicle with one arm through the open window, Jim and Dave at the back. When the car eased into the spot beside the gas pump, the driver held his empty wallet open for the men to inspect. Jim chuckled under his breath and looked over at Dave to see if he had caught on.

"What kind of place is this? Is everyone hanging on by a thread?"

```
BILL:    You should probably mention that any
         vehicle driving down the road is a
         potential ride.

PETE:    You can say that you just wave your
         hand over the road. Don't flap your
         arm like you're an eagle or anything,
         just gently lift it up and down, and a
         car will stop for you and take you to
         your destination.

JOANNA: I remember we took a car home once,
        Pete and I, and one of the wheels
        fell completely off, so we
        abandoned the car along the side of
        the road, and we walked the rest of
```

the way home. I thought that was kind
of funny.

PETE: I don't think we paid that guy
        actually.

LORI: Okay, I got it.

Jim handed over a few crisp bills to their driver, who took

them over to the clerk in the center of the station, and soon they

were on their way again only to be greeted a half a mile down the

road by a small herd of cattle on the search for their evening

rations in the alleys, cabbage cast-offs and the thicker grass that

grew along the edge of the dumpsters. Traffic came to a stop,

providing another chance for Dave to offer his two cents.

MARY: *(jumping up from her spot on the sofa)*
        Oh, I remember that time when Dave
        came with Grandpa! I think I gave up
        my bed for one of them.

BILL: On their first morning, I got up
        before everyone else to get the
        breakfast ready, and I found Dave in
        the dining area with coffee cup in
        hand, ready to debrief on his first
        day in the country.

LORI: When they came, our senses were
        heightened. We saw people and places
        from their point of view.

MARY: Remember when we first got there? The
        families who got there before —they

```
               had to explain everything to us.
               They'd say, "This is normal. Don't be
               surprised." That's what we had to
               say to Grandpa a lot.

LORI:          (laughing) I think I lost where I was.
               (finding her place in the manuscript)
               Oh, here we are -talking about the
               building project.
```

The building project was a pole-barn structure, and Jim was determined to make every working-minute count. Being of service to his son-in-law was top priority for he could see the stress in Bill's face and the way his shoulders weighed down with the worries of gathering all the materials.

"Bill just came from the north, from a city near the Russian border with all of this wood," Jim remarked to his companion.

"I don't know how he managed it," Dave chimed in.

"He bribed, I mean...he gave gifts to the manager of the sawmill, to make sure that they gave him good, wide boards and then he brought it all here by train."

Dave pointed to the lumber stacked on the cement foundation. "So, they made all those two-by-eights and two-by-fours by hand?"

"Yes, but then the saw gave out—so there won't be any more boards until we get a new pulley."

"What about the one you brought with you in your carry-on?" Dave asked.

Jim took the pulley from his jean pocket, "Wouldn't you know I brought the wrong size. Bill forgot to mention that they work in metric over here. We hope to hunt one down this afternoon in the Material District. We won't be gone long."

But they were.

MARY: Grandpa and Dave worked really, really hard. Grandpa might have been tired or impatient, but he never complained. And he had his cute side-ways smile…

JOANNA: …And always wore his French beret driving hat. I was so proud to show off my grandfather to all my friends. He was our connection to family since he was the only one to visit us.

PETE: Grandma came at the end. Uncle Don too.

MARY: I loved the gifts that Grandpa brought us. Don't you remember the black Lisa Frank T-shirt with the rainbow-colored Dalmatian on it? It was so amazing.

JOANNA: I think you wore that shirt every day for a year.

MARY: Shh! Let Mom read.

Unfortunately, the only pulley that Bill and Jim could find in the boxes of greasy hardware was a used one and the key that should hold it onto the shaft was missing. But they paid for it and returned to the building site where Jim disappeared around the side of the building.

It was quiet for the first moments as Jim pulled a length of old wire from the fencing at the back of the property. Then there was the sound of metal hitting metal as he fashioned a square-key for the pulley himself.

"This might do it," he said holding up the key pounded out of thick wire.

"But that stack of lumber is awfully green and wet. Think it will hold up?" Dave asked.

"We'll see," Jim said, joining Bill at the table saw.

However, their work would have to wait. A ferocious dogfight flared up at the base of the construction. The men stationed on the second floor leaned over to watch as two dogs growled and snapped at each other with the intensity of life and death. When one dog left limping and bloody, they turned back to the saw. Bill inserted the pulley with its improvised key and the belt whirled around. The men let out a cheer.

BILL: Jim would've made a good missionary, making something out of nothing.

PETE: It wasn't all work. Didn't we all escape to the countryside with Grandpa and Dave? I mean to the dinosaur resort?

JOANNA: *(with feeling)* That trip should've been called "The Weekend of the Sour Cabbage Soup."

MARY: Yeah, we went with your youth group, and you guys got to sleep *inside* where it was warm, but I had to stay in the cold with Grandpa and Dave in a *gher*. I remember the night sky was black and the stars were so bright. Grandpa got up in the night several times to keep the fire going in the wood stove, but the fire went completely out—so he took the rug right off the floor to cover up with.

JOANNA: We were going to play a trick on you since we knew you were scared to sleep out there. It was going to be the shaving cream joke.

MARY: But Grandpa caught onto you and told you guys to get back to bed. He protected me. Really, I was such a scattered brained, whacka-doodle kid, but I felt so peaceful around him. He was there for me too, not just for Dad.

PETE: *(with a sly smile)* Mom, ya' taking notes?

At breakfast, just before the group left the resort, one youth nearly shouted over the tops of the patrons' heads. "How are we supposed to eat this?"

In front of each person was a plate of overly-salted meat, cabbage, and rice. "Wasn't the sour soup torture enough?" said another.

"You'll be hungry if you don't eat," Grandpa told them.

The teens washed their hands of the whole thing and headed for the Russian van, their connection to civilization and kiosks with candy bars.

With everyone inside, the driver announced that the vehicle wouldn't start and that they would have to push it down the side of the incline toward the road.

"You're serious?" Dave gasped, his eyes on the steep terrain.

Jim and Dave joined the teens at the back of the van to push it down the grassy, mountainous slope. In the driver's seat, Bill popped the clutch and the engine chugged, rumbled, and started. Everyone rushed down the hill to catch up to the vehicle, all anxious to get home.

At the bottom of the next valley, the van stalled again. This time, Dave offered to walk up the road for some help. He returned with a Japanese tourist and his SUV. The gentlemen seemed to understand the predicament despite the lack of a common language, and the Japanese pulled the group up and out.

BILL: The van stalled several times on that trip. We had to let it coast in neutral down into a farmer's field, and he helped us to get on the road.

PETE: I kind of remember it was a common theme of every trip, so I don't remember any details.

LORI: Listen up, guys. We're at the end.

By the time the two men left Ulaanbaatar, two floors were framed. Dave had a welt on the side of his head from a hefty two-by-eight that fell on him and arms full of stories to tell his wife.

```
PETE:   Hey, how long did that key hold up?

BILL:   As far as I can remember, it held up
        until the building was finished.

MARY:   Grandpa would call that a miracle.
```

On the morning when the pair left the building site for the airport, the crane towered above the work site, ready to lift the huge trusses into place on top of the framing.

With the city getting smaller and smaller behind them, Dave remarked, "It was a good trip, wasn't it?"

With tears in his eyes, Jim answered, "It was sure worth it."

```
JOANNA:   It's good, Mom. We love it.
```

Go with the Flow

Bill in the northwestern corner of Övörkhangai Province
Karakorum, the Old Capital
Uugii Nuur (Uugii Lake)

The sun emerges in brilliant red, a spectacular send-off for the men bound for the best fishing lake in the country. Bill's job is to secure the wooden rowboat on the top of the van. He threads the rope through the metal hooks and uses a knot mastered in his youth on the lakes of Minnesota. Though the sky brightens by the minute, Bill can't shake the sense of doom that accompanies every trip to the countryside.

Yesterday, while he and Bataraa the company driver replaced the old tires, he reflected on how most trips ended. If he had his way, Bill would fill the back of the van with a variety of engine parts, a month's supply of beef jerky, a medical emergency kit, and in his pocket---cash for bribes. In mission training, his instructors emphasized the value of describing all possible outcomes when making plans. They called this the "work of worry."

"Who's ready?" Tom cheers from behind a camcorder, his wiry body buried in a dark blue sweatshirt with UCLA splashed across the front. Bill admires his friend's "anything-goes" attitude, wishing it would rub off on him. The camera points in Bill's direction, so he gives his friend a reluctant nod.

At the back of the van, Bill's son Pete uses his body weight to hold back a mass of fishing gear, the cooler, the tent, and the .22 rifle. Hanging from his arm is a plastic bag bulging with candy bars. "I've got the Snickers!" he yells and spins around quickly to slam the back door on their supplies.

A shout comes from the left, "Do we have enough toilet paper?" Tom's son James strides toward the van shielding his face from the camera. "Someone always gets the runs."

Ah, refreshing! Bill is glad he isn't the only one who wants to be ready for everything.

Inside the van, Tom's oldest son Ryan smooths the hair out of his eyes and kicks a box of Pepsi under the backseat. "To control its consumption," he says.

The camera is aimed at Bill again, Tom asks, "So, where is this fine bunch of men headed for this time?"

Bill blows warm air into his hands. Though it's mid-June, the temperature dipped into the 40s overnight. He slides his hands into his pockets and plays along with Tom's spoof on the *Red Green Show*. "Our destination is Uughii Nuur, a legendary lake in the grasslands of northwest Mongolia. And should I mention the only lake for hundreds of miles? Where only the brave venture? Not to worry, we have a Russian tin can and an expert driver."

Bill remembers the winter hunting trip with their driver Bataraa. He used duct tape to repair a rotting radiator and squeezed more miles from one liter of gas than physically possible. Every man they met claimed to be hunting guides, all eager to check out his 30-ought six. On that trip, they started with five men but returned with thirteen. One of them was apprehensive every single minute.

"Uughii Nuur? Sounds exotic," Tom prompts.

"We've never traveled in that direction before and there are no roads to get there, but if we're lucky we'll arrive by sundown."

"Let's go then," Tom shouts and the six crowd into the van. They bounce out of the yard and descend the steep gravel road to the highway that follows the river.

Their first stop: the ruins of Karakorum, the original center of Genghis Khan's empire. Bill surveys the stone fortress, trying to imagine the leader of the vast Mongol empire, crossing the threshold of the main gate. With the north wind picking up considerably, their video recording becomes a humorous pantomime of Tom holding onto his baseball cap, motioning over his shoulder at the stone turtle and the architectural stupas that march in a perfect line on the grassy slope. Though no one can hear him, he begins his monologue with, "Six hundred years ago..."

With each mile, another layer of dust collects on the windshield. The van jostles along the path, sending its passengers forward and back and from side to side. Bill's head slams against the window. He feels for a bump on his temple and the rowboat squeaks and scrapes the roof above him making him wish they had never taken it. Sure that the boat is slipping, he insists they stop and tighten the ropes.

Getting out, Ryan remarks that it feels good to stretch their legs, and Bataraa sweeps the front window with a little broom.

Several hours into the day the ruts disappear and a vote is taken to choose the way. The one they choose is an open stretch and comparatively smooth, leading them higher and further north. When a lone yurt comes into view, Bataraa says, "We'll stop and ask about the lake."

The housewife comes out of the yurt wearing the knee-length dress of the centuries called the *del*. Her face is sunburned and leathery, and her smile reveals teeth as white as the hard cheese drying in a wooden crate on the roof of her home. "Uughii Nuur? I've never heard of it."

"We're still in Övörkhangai Province, aren't we?" the driver is seeking reassurance.

"Of course, but there's no lake anywhere that I know of," she says and sweeps her hand across the horizon.

With the risk of being rude, they refuse the customary milk tea and chatting. They point the van west. At nightfall, Bataraa pulls the van to a stop on a flat piece of pasture absent of rocks. He turns off the headlights to save the battery. In complete darkness, the younger men pull out the sleeping bags and stretch out under the stars while the older three curl up in the van, cramped, but out of the cold.

Morning dawns with a sky of milky purple, and Bill creeps out of the van and shuts the door gently behind him. A strange stillness in the air amplifies the sound of animals murmuring. He looks around. It appears a herd of sheep snuggled up to the boys in the middle of night, and a yurt is less than fifty yards away!

Bill sees smoke rising from the stovepipe of the humble dwelling. No doubt, a family is preparing breakfast on the wood stove in the center of their home. Bill and the other men will be their guests for doughnut holes and tea.

Back on the journey, the boys entertain each other with burping and long descriptions of where to purchase a decent pair of shoes. Bill must admit he enjoys their uninhibited conversation. Then, without warning, a village of wooden houses appears. The first building they approach is a shed with a serendipitous fuel pump where they meet an older gentleman who has stopped by for some cigarettes.

He knows the way. "Go between those two hills to the west. Can you see them? Keep going and you'll find it."

The endless fields pass by, and Bill worries if all this lurching back and forth hasn't done some real damage. Perhaps his boat, designed and constructed by his friend Tim Purnell, will never have a second try. Memories of its maiden voyage will have to be enough.

Christened *Pike Fever*, he and Tim had launched it into the frigid depths of the Tuul River with plenty of congratulations from their wives. The boat floated—that's what mattered most. The deep, black water swept the two men towards their destination. Along the way, city folk enjoying the warm weather held up bottles of vodka as they passed, and some stripped down to their waists to hale down a ride. Bill smiles at the memory, and holds on to the strap above his head as the van takes a sharp turn.

Before noon, Uughii Nuur stretches out in front of them like a huge mirror reflecting the clouds and the blue sky above. This three-mile lake is teeming with northern pike, yellow perch, and Siberian taimen, the most coveted catch with its record-breaking size and mouth of sharp teeth.

The moment the van stops, the boat flies off the van and goes into the water with a splash and a shout. The teenagers play at fishing, build fires, and eat as many peanut butter sandwiches as they can make.

The second day brings what Bill calls "true success." The yellow spoon with its five, red dots does its job as Pete appears to have a large fish on the line.

"Hold on! He'll give you a fight!" Bill yells.

Just as soon as Pete pulls the fish to shore, his catch takes off with lightning speed toward the deep. Pete struggles to keep his feet on the ground and is dragged into the water. He digs his heels into the sandy soil, and Bill holds him by the waist. Pete must hoist the fish to shore two more times before the fish exhausts himself and succumbs.

The men huddle around as the creature writhes and twists under the strength of Pete's arms. Then, Bill runs for the measuring tape with a feeling of euphoria, and Tom grabs the camera.

Pete's northern pike measures well over a meter and weighs in at nineteen pounds. Bill looks up from gutting the prize fish to see two ranchers stop by on horseback to see how the foreigners are faring. If he has heard correctly, they are offering their daughters as brides for the young men. Dismounting, the two men say their daughters are prettier than the girls of the city. Everyone laughs.

There is fried fish for lunch with cold bread and Pepsi for everyone. One of the ranchers volunteers to  demonstrate the art of marmot hunting. Even James crawls on his belly with the rifle dragging beside him. He twirls a white handkerchief over his head and moves closer and closer toward the prey.

To end the day, the sun-kissed men watch the visitors prepare barbecue the traditional way. After cleaning the marmot, they return the meat to steam in its own skin. Using a long stick, they turn the meat over the fire in quick little movements.

The men listen to the fur sizzle and watch the carcass blow up to the size of a basketball. The dark meat bursts in their mouth with a unique flavor, but Tom can't resist, "Tastes like chicken, doesn't it?"

Smiles are as wide as the lake. Bill wipes his mouth with his sleeve, and the visitors say good night with candy bars tucked in their riding jackets. The horses kick up the dirt as they leave to the west. With the sound of their pounding of their hooves on the steppes, Bill wonders if Genghis Khan ate with his men on this very spot.

The third day looms dark, gray and threatening. Blustery winds make securing the boat to the van more than a challenge. The rendezvous with nature must come to an end, but it's not without an encore. The skies let loose with a torrential rain.

Strangely enough, though the van slides through the mire, Bill feels considerably lighter on his way home.

About fifty miles from home, Pete yells out, "Do you smell something?" Steam fills the interior of the van, and Bataraa confesses that the duct tape on the radiator hose is a year old. So, he waits for the engine to cool down and he adds several more layers of tape. The men's hot breath fogs the windows, but with a swish of their sleeves, they're off.

Just a quarter mile short of home, the van struggles to make it up the last hill. They will walk the rest of the way, leaving Bataraa to watch their things until they can return with the car. It drizzles now, but Bill doesn't notice. In front of him, the boys race to the top of the hill. With each step, he takes a mental inventory. There are no extra passengers, no injuries, no regrets.

Returning

Southeast Missouri, Summer 2007
References to the Mongolian countryside and to the hills outside
of Gants Hudag near our home, February 2000

"Dad hasn't been on an airplane since we got back from Mongolia," Mary announces twenty miles short of the airport, her huge pink suitcase in the backseat.

Mother takes her eyes off the road and manages a quick smile in her daughter's direction.

"You're sure you have everything? Five months is a long time."

"I'm okay, Mom. Stop worrying."

The pair journeys a few miles in silence when a small flock of blackbirds joins them on Mary's side of the vehicle, the steady stroke of their wings somehow parallel to her determination to go out on her own. She watches them thoughtfully until they flew off to the east. "Do you remember how I used to be so afraid of blackbirds?"

"I should *never* have let you watch that Agatha Christie mystery, the one with the murder with the clothesline."

"Yeah, but I mean the blackbirds I saw with Tsatsanna on the day I picked out my goats."

"Remind me."

At dinner one evening, Mary announced to her family that she wanted to keep goats. "We have plenty of hay." She bulldozed ahead before anyone could protest. "Tsatsanna said her family has lots of goats just two hours from here, and her brother Sukhbaatar will let me take my pick. I already asked him."

"You did, did you?" Dad said from his end of the table. "You'll have to take them to the meadows every day until school starts. He pointed toward the pastures on the hills above their neighborhood. "In fact, you'll have to sit with them most of the day, 'cause if you don't, they won't be fat enough for winter."

Mary understood her part of the bargain. She also knew her best friend would keep her company and that Tsagaa would help.

The day for choosing the goats arrived. In the coatroom by the front door, Mary listened to the last-minute lecture about responsibility and commitment and agreed to return the goats to their rightful owners in the fall. With that, Dad left to service the van and to fill the tank.

Before too long, Tsatsanna arrived at the door with two canteens of food. "My sister made fried meat pancakes...and potato salad!"

"And I brought mandarin oranges and *oondaa* for both of us. Grape. It's the best!"

Soon, the two age-mates ran hand in hand through the gate. They were on their way to the countryside where her friend's family lived in the traditional way, migrating with their animals from one pasture to another.

"All of our goats are cute, and the sheep are too. But it's hard to tell them apart, so I'll help you!" Tsatanna said.

At the toll bridge to Turtle Rock, while the grown-ups submitted their identification papers to the police, the two girls roamed the rocky hillside to look for wildflowers. The sun was as bright as ever, the air fresh and sweet. They descended the hill with their hands full, and Mary's mother motioned for them to pose for a photograph on the bridge. The two girls stood so close together that their bouquets merged into one at their waists.

Eventually, the van crested a hill that looked down on two yurts of weathered sheep wool. Smoke ascended from the pipe from the top of the larger one. At the top of the yurt, a flap of wool lay back on itself, an opening for light and for cooking.

A lively bunch of goats and sheep roamed the hill behind the yurts, and just as her friend had said, the goats were hard to distinguish from the sheep. Every head had horns whether male or female and sported several amazing shades of red, brown and black. They bleated out frightened greetings as Mary made steps in their direction. She had just begun to study them when the guests from the city were called into the yurt for preliminaries.

First, they must sit through the hospitality rituals. First on the list, they must drink milk tea from blue and white porcelain bowls, not Mary's favorite part. Then, they must dip doughnut holes into the hot liquid and suck on them, while the men passed the snuff bottle and pretended to sniff the sweet tobacco.

They must say, "*It's good.*" Cousins would roll out dough for noodles, and mutton would be chopped and added to the large wok at the center of the yurt while family photos were passed from one guest to another.

With the meal complete, Mary realized she hadn't used the toilet for several hours. However, when she left the group to explore the outhouse, she was disappointed to find the three-walled structure just like the one she had nearly fallen into the previous summer. Unable to shake the fear of the open hole in the ground, she decided against using it and ran toward the herd. Tsatsanna's older cousins followed closely on her heels.

"Look at that little one. He's the color of peanut butter! What a cute creature!" Mary said, mildly aware of the charming her native pronunciation had on the cousins.

The oldest boy explained, "The little ones are still nursing. We can't separate them from their mothers."

Mother interrupts the storytelling. "But we took those young ones home with us, didn't we?"

"Yeah, Sukhbaatar said if we take the babies *and* their mothers it would be okay."

"That's right. But what about the blackbirds? Stories with you take forever. There's only twenty minutes to our exit."

"After we chose the animals, Dad secured ropes around their necks and used them like leashes. They were too afraid to get in the van. They put up such a fight. Just when we thought we were ready to go, Dad was called over to make a proper visit to the old grandmother in the second yurt. Remember?"

"Oh, yeah."

"Well, while you and daddy were busy visiting, Tsatsanna and I went out exploring. We found an *ovo* where the Mongols place rocks and where they hang the blue scarves for the spirits of the mountain. Tsatsanna walked around the pile of rocks clockwise three times, just like she's supposed to, when suddenly a flock of blackbirds whipped up out of nowhere, and I ran away as fast as I could. When I stopped and looked back, the birds were still there hovering on the ground near the *ovo.*"

"It's all coming back to me. But if you were so afraid of blackbirds, why are they such a comfort now?" Mother asks.

"Remember the mountain that Tsatsanna and I liked to

climb? The one on the other side of the landfill? From the top, we could watch the busses making their turns and stops. From one angle, we could see the whole north section of the capital city. If we faced the east, we could see the prison and the military training camp."

"I didn't know you went up there. This is sounding more and more like a confession. You shouldn't have roamed so far."

"Hold on, the good part is coming. When Daddy broke the news to us that we were leaving to go back to the States, I needed to climb it one more time. So, I took Tsatsanna up there with me. We took the most direct route but it went through the area where families dumped their trash, mostly bottles and plastic and remains of animal carcasses. Even with all that trash around me, I couldn't help but remember so many wonderful things about my life there. I remembered how I had traditional shoulder dancing lessons, and how much I enjoyed making meat dumplings with the women. My heart was so full of memories that I thought it might burst. I didn't want to leave."

"My heart was broken too,'" Mother interjects. "Remember our first year back in the States? If you and I tried to speak Mongolian with each other, one of us would start choking up in the middle of a sentence."

"We were almost near the top when some blackbirds flew up out of the valley. They landed really close to where the two of us sat on the rocks. I sat perfectly still. For some reason, I didn't run away. My heart beat so hard. I know this sounds corny but it was like God came really close to me. I felt like he was saying, 'Don't be afraid. Whenever you see these blackbirds, remember I will never leave you.'"

Mary takes a sip of her water bottle and continues, "I had so many questions about what my future would look like. I didn't know where we would live or what would happen next, but as I watched those blackbirds, I felt such an incredible peace."

On the exit ramp to Highway 70 just a few miles short of the airport, Mother says, "Things turned out okay, didn't they?"

"They've been good years. But now I'm ready to go," Mary replies.

Mother merges the vehicle into a long string of cars. "I'm going to miss you."

They pass under the sign designated for *Departures*.

Mary says, "I've always wanted to do this."

"I know. And you should."

APPENDIX

The Younker's 12 Stones
February 2000

As an exercise of gratitude, Bill sat the family down for a special discussion that he called the 'Twelve Stones.' Pete age 16, Joanna age 14, and Mary age 10 listened intently as their father described how Joshua, the Old Testament leader of the Hebrews, took the Israelites across the Jordan River on dry ground to the Promised Land. Joshua instructed the leaders of the 12 tribes to *each* take a stone as a memorial for future generations. The Goal? To remember God's deliverance.

So, we decided we would choose 12 people, places, or events that expressed God's provision in our lives in Mongolia. This unique time of reminiscing and thanking the Lord was precious. Because of our time together in Mongolia, we are all closer to the Lord and to each other. This wonderful experience –although mixed with sorrows, good-byes, fires, robberies, and disappointments—has changed us forever.

At the time of this publication, Pete is a youth pastor with his wife Kimber and their three children in NW Iowa, Joanna is a primary care physician and Mary is a woman of business and art. Both reside on the Treasure Coast of Florida (where it's warm).

#1 Our team members

The Suchys:
Tom, Lynn and their four children were more than family to us. Fellowshipping on Friday evenings with prayer, singing, sharing, and even a game was a highlight of the week.

The Watkins.
Steve and Donna became like grandparents for our children and always had words of encouragement for each one of us.

The Shooks:
Tom, Gayle, Ryan, Joy, and James joined our team in 1998. It was so nice to have teens on the team. They were a fun family to serve with. Most of our adventures as a whole family included the Shook family.

The Sprengers:
This amazing family –Mike and Carol Beth and their children– arrived in 1999.Their addition to our team and to the homeschooling community was immeasurable. What a delight to have them in our lives even to this day. Their time in Mongolia stretched nearly three times the length of ours.

Laurel Sprenger's first-hand experience of the Mongolian life especially prepared her for her works of art included in this collection of memories.

#2   Our first house helper Munkhsoyol
From 1995-1997, B. Munksoyol became like a sister to Lori and was the sole reason Lori survived the first two years. From cleaning and shopping to cooking and advising, Soyoloh was there for us. With a pleasant personality—trustworthy and dependable—she helped us with all of our daily tasks and played with our children.

#3 Friends in the youth group
"It's tough without friends who speak English," says Pete. "So, friends from the youth group made a big difference." Pete remembers overnights with Justin, Marty, Austin, Dwight, and James. While Joanna especially appreciated Staci, her schoolmate as well. "Staci is a godly, caring, loving, faithful friend."

#4 Boldbaatar
Overall, working with him was fruitful. It was a privilege to guide him, to assist with his wedding and to see his family grow. We will always remember Boldbaatar, Dorjhand, Ariun Ilt and Enkrimaa.

#5 The Sukhbaatar family

Without the Sukhbaatar family there would be no house, no doors, no furniture, no greenhouse, no fence, no barn, no cabin. Sukhbaatar watched over his family: Anna (our first helper in Gants Hudag), Sara her sister (who assisted in sewing projects for Lori), Sukhchaluun, Tsatsanna, and Sukherhden (the youngest).

Tsatsanna, Mary's Mongolian friend. "She gave joy to my life," says Mary. We also know that she gave Mary the gift of Mongolian language by playing for hours each week.

#6 Boldbaatar Beef

This accidental success began with Pete and Bill in the kitchen of our first apartment. Eventually, by training one man in the butchering business, six church leaders had steady work. Each felt ready to choose a wife and to begin their families. Bold, Tsolmon, Toktaa, Tsaganna, Nandah, and Otbayer.

#7 Bor's family

Sharing a birthday with little Orna brought our two families together again and again. Celebrating Tsagaan Sar in Bor's home was always a treat. She opened her heart and home to me, her daughters are forever cherished.

#8 Working with Youth Builders on the mini-golf course

The opportunity to join the youth from the U.S. in the summer of 1999 was very meaningful to Jo and Pete. The addition of the mini-golf course was an amazing feat.

#9 Grandpa Gerdeen's visits

We all agree that having Lori's father visit each year was the highlight of the year. September 1995 included the famous fishing trip, September 1996 included eating in many Mongolian's homes, May 1998 with David Mahler with the work on the building, and October 1999 with Grandma, just for FUN!

#10 Housing changes

Each move was for the best. Moving to the Strub family's apartment while they were home in Germany meant more space, comfortable beds and warmth! Our straw-bale house gave us the following: "my own room!" "having horses," "big parties," "Pete's cabin," "Pickering's couch," "Warmth in subzero conditions," and "running hot water any time of year."

#11 The Homeschool Co-op

The homeschool co-operative was a blessing in a thousand ways. In the first year, we had 13 students, in the second year there were 22. Year 3 included all ages from preschool to high school with 60 students. Mrs. Marilyn Caden was our administrator for three years. Her family was very close to ours and spent many happy times together with us on the river (Peter, Justin, Chara).

Mike Sprenger joined us the last year. This was a blessing to our older students as he focused on spiritual guidance and training of the teens.

#12 Local food improvements

Those who live overseas are often obsessed with food. We get excited over peanut butter and the ability to produce the meals we enjoy in our homeland. Thus, we were all thrilled when Berlin Burger established itself in UB, even though the burger had shredded cabbage on it and the fries were always cold little pieces. Next came MFC for fried chicken. Then, Churchill's arrived in late 1998 which had fine service and real china dishes. New restaurants with good food snowballed in 1999 with City Coffee, El Toro, and Pizza de la Casa.

Special thanks to the Glen Reimer family, the John and Marnie Pickering family for opening their homes for dinner and Bible Study, sharing their expertise (teaching Joanna the flute) and the use of their horses and saddles when they were back in the States.

The Mongolian Hillbillies

Let us tell you a story 'bout a man named Bill,
Came from Minnesota, around the southern hills
Went hunting one day, shot at a blinded deer
And up from the ground came fifteen Mongol engineers
                  ...to help him hunt that is.

Well, they packed up their bags and moved to Mongolee
They took 'em to the airport and the man said, "No Siree"
They took 'em to the train but it left before they came...
So they traveled through the Gobi on a camel train.
                  ...delayed that is.

When they got to Mongolee, O' Bill he built a house of straw
In spite of the officials saying it may be against the law
Well the big bad wolf, he never blew it down
But someone took their saddles and cleared right out of town.
                  ...stolen that is.

His good wife Lori, was a Proverbs 31 as you can find,
She organized a material sale, with tickets, rules, and lines
When the gates were finally open, and the goods were to be sold
The lines went out the window and she turned to riot control.
                  ...chaos that is.

Their oldest boy Pete decided sisters were a pain,
So he moved out on his own and built his own house down the lane,
Joanna sang at Oz where she won *LaPorta's heart,
So he let her borrow videos which he usually would not part,
                  ...with, that is.

(continued on the next page)

The youngest was a learner, Mongolian she learned to speak
She had friends with which she played,
in the yard and down the street.
But Mary, she was a speedster, on the waterslide in Thai.
We'll always 'member her for hitting that boy with her eye...
.....rainbow colors that is.

So now it's time that we bid them all adieu.
Bill he goes to preaching, Lori back to school,
The kids they'll be enjoying going on a buying spree.
And we hope they never forget good ol' Mongoli
...ah, that is. We'll miss y'all.

Footnotes:

This song was written and song by Glen Reimer in harmony with Mike Sprenger at the goodbye party at the Homeschool Co-op, February 2000, Ulaanbaatar Mongolia.

*Mr. LaPorta was the ambassador of the United States who organized a musical for expatriates to perform on stage. Joanna was chosen for the part of Dorothy and won everyone's heart.

Special Thanks

I want to give special thanks to several who made the writing experience an enjoyable process. Cami Wheeler and Suzanne Pautler read, advised, and edited my stories. Their dialogue and encouragement trained me in the art of memoir. As well, my husband Bill, my parents, and the women of the Thursday morning writing circle gave me confidence to complete the project.

Winter 1994

Fall 2000

We would be remiss not to mention Lola and Don Hoes, our loving aunt and uncle, who graciously took in our family upon our return, providing us a place to rest and heal until we were situated in Missouri. Their home was a sanctuary, their love and acceptance never to be forgotten.

LORI YOUNKER, Author

Lori Younker and her husband Bill have made warm and woodsy Missouri their home since their return to the USA. Their children have grown and have started their careers as youth pastor (Pete), family physician (Joanna) and contracts/product manager (Mary). Lori has been a teacher of English for immigrants and as an adjunct instructor at Missouri University. Her husband Bill is the pastor of the International Community Church of Columbia, MO and their children flourish in their occupations, but will never forget the years they ventured together to the unknown.

Find Lori at **WorldSoBright.org** where she chronicles culture stories of all kinds and donates authors' fees to www.VisionTrust.org.

LAUREL SPRENGER, Illustrator

Laurel is a freelance artist and clothing designer. She works mainly with watercolor and pen & ink, but also enjoys acrylic and colored pencil. She specializes in portrait paintings. When she was three years old her family moved to Mongolia, where they lived in the city of Ulaanbaatar for twelve years. She then moved with her family to Thailand and stayed there for 3 years before moving back to her home state of Colorado, where she is currently working on gaining more skill and experience with her artwork and dressmaking. Contact Laurel by email at **laurelinartistry@gmail.com,** or with Instagram— **@LaurelinArtistry**